Fa
ENGLISH RECIPES

Traditional fare from around the counties

Illustrated with cottage scenes

SALMON

Index

Berkshire Jugged Steak 40
Buckinghamshire Rabbit Pie 19
Cheshire Soup 43
Cornish Pasty 13
Cumberland Sand Cake 31
Derbyshire Fruit Loaf 18
Devonshire Splits 45
Dorset Tea Bread 27
Durham Pikelets 39
Essex Meat Layer Pudding 21
Gloucester Pancakes 22
Hampshire Haslet 46
Hereford Apple Dumplings 10
Isle of Wight Doughnuts 34
Kentish Apple and Cheese Pie 47
Lancashire Hot Pot 29
Leicestershire Pudding 23
Norfolk Plough Pudding 32
Northamptonshire Cheesecakes 6
Northumbrian Girdle Cakes 11
Nottingham Pudding 42
Oxford Sausages 26
Rutland Savoury Cheese Custard 35
Shropshire Fidget Pie 38
Somerset Chicken 15
Staffordshire Beef Steaks 14
Suffolk Fish Pie 7
Surrey Lamb Pie 16
Sussex Sausage Rolls 8
Warwickshire Pheasant Casserole 3
Westmorland Parkin 5
Wiltshire Pork Pie 24
Worcestershire Baked Apple Pudding 30
Yorkshire Pudding 37

Cover pictures: *front:* Off to Market *by Helen Allingham*
back: Going out to Play *by Helen Allingham*
title page: A Thatched Cottage *by Arthur Claude Strachan*
Printed and Published by Dorrigo, Manchester, England

Warwickshire Pheasant Casserole

A brace of pheasants casseroled with red wine, brandy and sherry.

A brace of pheasant, prepared
A 'walnut' of butter
4 rashers back bacon, de-rinded and chopped
1 tablespoon flour
Salt and black pepper
¾ pint chicken stock
2 onions, peeled and chopped
1 carrot, peeled and sliced
4-6 small shallots, peeled and left whole
A bay leaf, two sprigs of parsley and a sprig of thyme, tied together with a piece of kitchen string
½ pint red wine
2 tablespoons brandy
6 oz button mushrooms, wiped

Melt the butter in a frying pan and quickly brown the pheasant on all sides. Remove from the pan and place in a casserole dish. Fry the bacon lightly in the residual butter, then stir in the flour and seasoning. Pour in the stock, stirring all the time. Add the onions, carrot and shallots and bring the mixture to the boil. Pour over the pheasant and add the *bouquet garni* of herbs. Set oven to 325°F or Mark 3. Pour the wine into the casserole, cover and cook for 2½-3 hours. Remove the herbs, add the brandy and mushrooms and cook for a further 30 minutes. Serve with creamed potatoes and a green vegetable. Serves 4.

Off for a Walk *by Myles Birket Foster*

Westmorland Parkin

Parkin, a form of gingerbread that contains oatmeal, is popular in the Northern Counties. It is firmer in texture than the more spongy gingerbread and should be kept a little while before being eaten.

1 lb porridge oats
8 oz flour
8 oz demerara sugar
1 teaspoon allspice
1 teaspoon salt
2 teaspoons baking powder
2 teaspoons ground ginger
1 lb black treacle
8 oz butter
1 teaspoon bicarbonate of soda
1 small egg, beaten
3 fl oz milk

Set oven to 350°F or Mark 4. Well grease and line a deep roasting tin 10 inches x 13 inches. Place all the dry ingredients into a large mixing bowl. Gently heat the treacle and butter together in a saucepan until melted and pour into the dry mixture. Stir well, add the beaten egg and stir again. Warm the milk, add it to mixture and beat well. Pour into the tin and bake for 1-1½ hours until firm. Leave in the tin for ½ hour then turn out on to a wire rack. Keep for 48 hours then cut into squares.

Northamptonshire Cheesecakes

The Midland shires have a considerable number of recipes for cheesecakes. This one is filled with a curd or cream cheese, fruit and almond mixture.

8 oz prepared shortcrust pastry
6 oz curd or cream cheese
2 oz butter
2 eggs
3oz caster sugar
4 oz currants
The finely grated rind of a lemon
A few drops of almond essence
A little ground nutmeg

Roll out the pastry on a lightly floured surface and use to line 14-16 lightly greased patty tins. Set oven to 350°F or Mark 4. In a bowl, beat the curd or cheese until smooth. Put the butter, eggs and sugar in a saucepan and heat gently, stirring, until thickened, but do not allow to boil. Remove from the heat and stir in the curd or cheese, then add the currants, lemon rind and almond essence. Combine well and fill the tins. Sprinkle a little nutmeg over each and bake for 20-25 minutes until well risen and golden. Serve hot or cold.

Suffolk Fish Pie

A simple-to-make and tasty supper dish.

2 lb cod or haddock fillets
1 pint milk
Salt and black pepper
3 hard boiled eggs, shelled
2 oz butter
2 oz flour
2 tablespoons chopped parsley
1 teaspoon chopped capers
1 lb mashed potatoes

Set oven to 375°F or Mark 5. Cook the fish in the milk in a saucepan, seasoning to taste. Reserve the milk and flake the fish. Butter a deep 2 to 2½ pint pie dish and put the fish into it. Slice the hard boiled eggs and lay on top of the fish. Melt the butter and stir in the flour, then add the reserved milk and cook, stirring, until thickened. Stir in the parsley and capers and season to taste. Pour this sauce over the fish and eggs. Cover with mashed potato, roughing it up lightly with a fork. Dot with a little butter and cook for 30 minutes or until the potato is lightly browned. Serve with a green vegetable, such as buttered spinach. Serves 4.

If desired, a layer of sliced tomato can be placed on top of the fish, before the potato topping is added.

Sussex Sausage Rolls

This is a very old recipe. These rolls make an ideal modern day hiker's lunch and it is recommended that they are eaten in the open air, preferably on the South Downs!

1¼ lb bread dough **1 lb sausages or sausagemeat**

First make the bread dough with strong white flour and yeast by the normal method. When prepared, cut off small pieces of dough and wrap them around each skinned sausage or the equivalent of sausagemeat rolled into a sausage shape. The dough should be ¼ inch-½ inch thick. Cover and leave to rise in a greased tin in a warm place for 20 minutes or until well risen. Bake at 425°F or Mark 7 for 15 minutes and then reduce the temperature to 350°F or Mark 4 for a further 20 minutes.

Drawing Water *by Helen Allingham*

Hereford Apple Dumplings

Apples, their centres filled with orange rind and currants, enclosed in pastry.

12 oz prepared shortcrust pastry
4 teaspoons sugar
4 cooking apples, peeled and cored
2 oz sultanas
Grated rind of half an orange
1 dessertspoon marmalade
¼ oz butter, softened
Milk and sugar for glazing

Set oven to 400°F or Mark 6. Roll out the pastry on a lightly floured surface and divide into 4 circles big enough to enclose the apples. Sprinkle each circle with a teaspoon of sugar and set an apple in the centre of each. Mix together the sultanas, orange rind, marmalade and butter and divide the mixture between the apples, filling the core hole. Bring the pastry up over the apples and seal firmly with a little water. Place the dumplings, upside-down, on a greased baking sheet and decorate the tops with any pastry trimmings, cut into leaves. Brush the dumplings with milk and sprinkle on a little sugar to glaze. Bake for 10 minutes, then reduce the oven temperature to 350°F or Mark 4 for a further 30 minutes or until the dumplings are golden brown. Serve with a little marmalade, warmed to make a sauce, or custard or cream. Serves 4.

Northumbrian Girdle Cakes

These cakes, containing currants, are also known as Gosforth Gridies.

1 lb self-raising flour
1 teaspoon salt
8 oz butter
4 oz sugar
4 oz currants
2 eggs, beaten
5 fl oz milk

Sift the flour and salt together in a bowl, then rub in the butter until the mixture resembles fine breadcrumbs. Add the sugar and currants, then make a well in the mixture and add the eggs and milk. Stir the mixture with a round-bladed knife until well-combined. Turn out on to a lightly floured surface and knead lightly, then roll out to approximately ½ inch thick. Cut into small rounds and bake on a hot, well-greased griddle or frying pan for 4-5 minutes on each side, until golden brown. Serve hot, with butter.

The Shepherd Boy *by Myles Birket Foster*

Cornish Pasty

The better quality the beef and the more finely cut the vegetables, the tastier will be the pasty.

PASTRY

1 lb flour	**Pinch of salt**
5 oz lard	**Water to mix**

FILLING

1 lb best lean beef	**1 small onion (optional)**
1 lb potatoes	**1 oz butter**
1 lb swede	**Pepper and salt to taste**

Set oven to 400°F or Mark 6. Make the pastry and divide into 4 equal pieces. Roll each piece into a round 7 inches in diameter. Cut up the potatoes into small, irregular shaped pieces, similarly the swede (and onion if used). Cut the beef into small cubes about ¼ inch square, removing all fat. On each round of pastry put a share of the vegetables and add the salt and pepper to taste. Then add the meat and a knob of butter and another sprinkle of pepper. Dampen the edges of the pastry and bring up from both sides with floured hands to envelope the filling. Pinch the edges together and crimp them firmly to seal. Cook on a floured baking tray for ¾ hour. Makes 4 pasties.

Staffordshire Beef Steaks

At the beginning of the 19th century, Mrs Maria Rundell's best-selling book A New System of Domestic Cookery *was published. It contained a number of regional recipes, including this one from Staffordshire.*

4 pieces of braising steak each approx. 4-6 oz
Salt and black pepper
½ oz flour
1 oz dripping
1 onion, peeled and sliced
¾ pint beef stock
1-2 tablespoons walnut ketchup

Flatten the steaks with a rolling pin, season with salt and pepper and dust with flour. Melt the dripping in a frying pan and fry the onion until golden. Add the steaks and brown on both sides. Pour the stock into the pan, cover and simmer for 1-1½ hours or until the steaks are tender. Stir in the walnut ketchup. Arrange the steaks, overlapping, on a heated serving dish and serve with the pan gravy poured over them, accompanied by creamed potatoes and a green vegetable. Serves 4.

Somerset Chicken

Braised chicken pieces combined with a tasty Somerset Cider and Cheddar cheese sauce.

4 chicken portions
2 oz butter
1 medium onion, peeled and diced
1 oz flour
¾ pint milk
¼ pint dry Somerset cider
4 oz Cheddar cheese, grated
1 level teaspoon made English mustard
Salt and pepper

Set oven to 350°F or Mark 4. Melt half the butter in a frying pan and lightly brown the chicken pieces. Transfer to a casserole dish and roast for approximately 1 hour until cooked through. Prepare the sauce by melting the remaining 1 oz butter in a saucepan and gently cooking the onion until soft and transparent. Stir in the flour and cook gently for 2-3 minutes, stirring all the time. Remove the pan from the heat and gradually stir in all the milk and cider. Return to the heat and bring to the boil, stirring all the time until the sauce thickens. Cook for 2-3 minutes. Remove from the heat and stir in threequarters of the cheese, the mustard and salt and pepper to taste. Pour the sauce over the cooked chicken, sprinkle with the remaining cheese and brown in a hot oven or under a grill. Serve hot with green vegetables and jacket potatoes.

Surrey Lamb Pie

Originally this pie was made with mutton chops and topped with a thick layer of sliced mushrooms, rather than with pastry.

8 small lamb chops, trimmed
Seasoned flour for dusting
1 oz butter or oil
2 onions, peeled and sliced
2 to 3 lamb kidneys, cored and sliced
Salt and black pepper
1 sprig fresh mint or 1 sprig fresh rosemary
½ pint lamb stock
4-8 oz mushrooms, wiped, trimmed and sliced
8 oz pastry (shortcrust or puff)

Set oven to 350°F or Mark 4. Dust the chops generously with seasoned flour. Heat the butter or oil in a frying pan and brown the chops on both sides. Arrange in a 2 pint pie dish and sprinkle the onions on top. Add the kidneys and season lightly, then add the sprig of mint or rosemary. Pour the stock into the frying pan and heat through, stirring to take up the residue of seasoned flour, then pour sufficient over the pie filling just to cover. Arrange the mushrooms in overlapping layers to cover the filling. Roll out the pastry and cover the pie; decorate with the trimmings. Glaze with milk or beaten egg and cook for about 40 minutes or until the pastry is crisp and golden. Serve with potatoes, carrots and a green vegetable. Serves 4.

Wash Day *by Helen Allingham*

Derbyshire Fruit Loaf

There are many fruit loaf recipes. This one, flavoured with marmalade, comes from the Peak District.

1 lb mixed dried fruit
8 oz sugar
½ pint hot tea
1 egg
1 lb self-raising flour
½ teaspoon mixed spice
½ teaspoon grated nutmeg
2 tablespoons marmalade

Put the dried fruit and the sugar into a mixing bowl, add the hot tea and leave to soak overnight. Next day, set oven to 300°F or Mark 2. Grease and line a 7 inch cake tin or two 1 lb loaf tins. Stir the egg, flour, spices and the marmalade into the fruit, sugar and tea mixture. Pour into the cake tin or the loaf tins. Bake for 1½ to 2 hours until firm to the touch or until a skewer pushed into the cake comes out clean. Do not open the oven during the first hour of baking time. This cake will keep well.

Buckinghamshire Rabbit Pie

A puff pastry pie with rabbit, cheese, macaroni and double cream.

A 2-2½ lb rabbit, jointed
A bouquet garni
1 onion peeled and stuck with 6 cloves
Salt and black pepper
1 small onion, peeled and finely chopped
2 oz short cut macaroni
2 oz Cheddar cheese, grated
2 teaspoons chopped fresh parsley
1 teaspoon chopped fresh thyme
½ pint double cream
8 oz prepared puff pastry
A little beaten egg

Soak rabbit joints in cold salted water for 1½ hours. Drain well. Place in a saucepan, cover with fresh water and bring to boil. Skim, then add *bouquet garni*, onion and seasoning. Cover and simmer for 1-1½ hours, until rabbit is tender. Remove rabbit, strain and reserve stock. Allow rabbit to cool slightly, then remove meat from the bones. Bring stock to the boil and add macaroni. Boil until tender, then drain macaroni and mix with rabbit meat. Stir in chopped onion, grated cheese and herbs and season. Turn rabbit mixture into a 2 pint pie dish with a pie funnel. Pour over the cream. Set oven to 425°F or Mark 7. Roll out pastry, line rim of dish with a narrow strip, brush with cold water and top with remaining pastry; trim edges and press down. Cut steam vents, then brush with beaten egg. Bake for 40 minutes or until golden brown. Serve with creamed potatoes and carrots. Serves 4-6.

Children Playing *by Henry John Sylvester Stannard*

Essex Meat Layer Pudding

A filling and warming winter luncheon dish.

SUET PASTRY

6 oz flour **¼ teaspoon salt** **3 oz shredded suet** **½ cup cold water**

FILLING

1 tablespoon butter
2 medium onions, sliced
8 oz minced pork
8 oz minced chicken
1 teaspoon dried sage
¼ teaspoon dried oregano
1 tablespn chopped chives
¼ teaspoon celery salt
Salt and black pepper
1 tablespoon flour
2 egg yolks
2 tablespns double cream

Pastry: sift the flour and salt into bowl and mix in suet. Add enough water to make stiff dough. Wrap and put in refrigerator for 10 minutes. Meanwhile make filling. Fry onions in butter until golden. Add meats, herbs, seasonings and flour. Mix well, cook for 5 minutes then remove pan from heat. Beat together egg yolks and cream and add to meat mixture. Cook 5 minutes more. Butter 2½ pint pudding basin. Roll out dough to ¼ inch thick. Cut circle to fit bottom of basin and put in place. Spoon on layer of meat mixture (about 1½ inches deep) then add another circle of dough to fit and another layer of meat. Continue, finishing with layer of dough. Ingredients will not fill basin; dough needs room to expand. Cover basin and steam for 4 hours. Turn out and serve with vegetables. Serves 4.

Gloucester Pancakes

This Cotswold pudding is not prepared with a batter, but with a suet dough and it is the suet that gives the pancakes their attractive 'sandy' texture.

6 oz flour
Pinch of salt
1 level teaspoon baking powder
3 oz shredded suet
1 egg, beaten
A little milk
Lard for frying

Stir together the flour, salt and baking powder in a bowl then rub in the suet. Add the egg and sufficient milk to produce a stiff dough. Roll out on a lightly floured surface to about ½ inch thick, then cut into about 12 rounds, using a plain (not fluted) 2 inch cutter. Melt a little lard in a frying pan and fry the cakes until golden brown on both sides. Drain well and serve at once with warmed golden syrup or a lemon sauce. Makes about 12 cakes.

Leicestershire Pudding

Also known as Hunting Pudding, there are a number of variations of this recipe, which dates back at least to the 18th century. As well as being served as part of a hearty meal after a day's hunting, this pudding was also sliced cold and taken as a snack to be eaten on the hunting field.

8 oz seedless raisins
4 oz flour
4 oz shredded suet
2 eggs, beaten
1 teaspoon grated lemon rind
1 teaspoon ground nutmeg
1 fl oz brandy
Milk

In a bowl, mix together the raisins, flour and suet, then stir in the eggs, lemon rind, nutmeg and brandy, combining well. Add sufficient milk to make a stiff mixture and spoon into a well buttered 1½-2 pint pudding basin. Smooth over the top and cover with buttered greaseproof paper and kitchen foil and tie down securely. Place in a saucepan with sufficient boiling water to come half-way up the basin, cover and steam for 4 hours, adding more water as necessary. Turn out of the basin on to a warm serving dish and serve with brandy-flavoured whipped cream or custard. Serves 4. Traditionally this pudding was boiled in a well-floured cloth, making it ball-shaped, in old-fashioned Christmas Pudding style.

Wiltshire Pork Pie

The county of Wiltshire has always been famous for its pork products and this pie, which can be served hot or cold, makes an ideal packed lunch meal.

12 oz prepared shortcrust pastry
½ oz butter
1 onion, peeled and chopped
2 rashers streaky bacon, rind removed and chopped
1 lb belly of pork, chopped
1 small cooking apple, peeled and chopped
2-3 oz Cheddar cheese, diced
2 tablespoons chopped fresh parsley
1 teaspoon chopped fresh sage
Salt and black pepper
Pinch of dry mustard
1 egg, beaten
A small sprig of sage for garnish

Roll out pastry on a lightly floured surface. Divide in half and use half to line a lightly greased 9 inch pie plate. Melt butter in a frying pan and lightly fry onion and bacon. Add pork and cook for 15 to 20 minutes, stirring frequently. Allow to get cold, then stir in apple, cheese, herbs and seasoning, adding sufficient egg to bind the mixture. Set oven to 425°F or Mark 7. Fill pie plate with pork mixture and top with remaining pastry, sealing edges and trimming. Make a steam hole and decorate. Brush with remaining beaten egg to glaze. Bake for 15 minutes, then reduce temperature to 350°F or Mark 4 and bake for further 25 to 30 minutes, until golden brown. Serve hot or cold, garnished with sage. Serves 4 to 6.

Letting in the Cat *by Helen Allingham*

Oxford Sausages

The recipe for these skinless sausages dates back to the 18th century.

1 lb lean boneless pork
1 lb lean boneless English veal
12 oz shredded suet
8 oz fresh white breadcrumbs
Grated rind of half a lemon
1 teaspoon ground nutmeg
1 tablespoon chopped mixed fresh parsley, thyme, mint and marjoram
1 teaspoon chopped fresh sage
Salt and black pepper
1 egg, beaten
A little flour for dusting

Mince or *very* finely chop the pork and veal. Place in a large bowl and add the suet, breadcrumbs, lemon rind, nutmeg and all the herbs. Mix well together and season. Add the egg and stir well until the mixture is well combined and bound together. Flour the hands and form the mixture into sausage shapes. Dust lightly with flour and either cook the sausages under a hot grill, turning frequently until brown and cooked through, or fry in a mixture of oil and butter for about 8 minutes, turning frequently. Serve with creamed potatoes, grilled tomatoes and bacon. Makes approximately 24 sausages.

Dorset Tea Bread

In this recipe the 'tea' refers to the ingredient rather than to the meal at which it is served.

1 cup of tea
6 oz butter
8 oz soft brown sugar
12 oz mixed dried fruit (can include some walnuts, if liked)
12 oz self-raising wheatmeal flour
1 teaspoon ground mixed spice
1 teaspoon ground cinnamon
3 medium eggs, beaten

Set oven to 325°F or Mark 3. Put the tea, butter, sugar and fruit into a saucepan and simmer gently for 15 minutes until the fruit is plump. Cool slightly and beat in the flour, spices and eggs. Put into a greased and lined 8 inch diameter round cake tin and bake for 2 hours until cooked through and a skewer pushed in to the cake comes out clean. Turn out on to a wire rack to cool and serve sliced, plain or buttered, as preferred.

At the Cottage Gate *by Helen Allingham*

Lancashire Hot Pot

The name comes from the straight-sided earthenware dish in which the stew was traditionally cooked. There are many variations of Hot Pot recipes but all are 'thatched' with a layer of sliced potato.

2 lb middle end of neck of lamb, divided into 8 cutlets
1 oz lard or dripping
4 onions, peeled and sliced
2 lb potatoes, peeled and thinly sliced
4 carrots, peeled and sliced or ½ lb mushrooms, wiped and quartered
Salt and black pepper
2 pints lamb stock
Chopped fresh parsley to garnish

Set oven to 325°F or Mark 3. Trim any excess fat from the cutlets. Heat the lard or dripping in a frying pan and lightly brown the cutlets on both sides. In a large ovenproof casserole, layer up the cutlets, onions, carrots or mushrooms and potatoes, seasoning each layer successively, finishing with a neat 'thatch' of potatoes. Pour in the stock. Sprinkle a little salt over the potato 'thatch' and brush with melted lard or dripping. Cover and cook for 1½ to 2 hours. Remove from the oven and brush the potatoes with a little more melted lard or dripping and cook, uncovered, for a further 20 to 30 minutes until the potatoes are golden brown and crisp. Serve garnished with parsley and accompanied by pickled red cabbage or plain boiled red cabbage, if preferred. Serves 4.

Worcestershire Baked Apple Pudding

This recipe is more of a flan than a pudding – a pastry case filled with puréed apple topped with candied fruit.

2 cooking apples, peeled, cored and sliced
3 oz sugar
Grated rind and juice of ½ lemon
6 oz butter, softened to a cream
2 eggs
1 egg yolk
8 oz prepared shortcrust pastry
Candied lemon peel

Rinse the apples in cold water and place in a saucepan that has been rinsed in cold water. Add the sugar and simmer gently, stirring, until the apples are soft and pulpy. Sieve, then stir in the lemon rind and juice. Add the creamed butter and combine well. Beat the eggs and egg yolk together and strain into the apple mixture. Set oven to 375°F or Mark 5. Roll out the pastry on a lightly floured surface and use to line an 8 inch greased flan dish, trimming the edges neatly. Spoon in the apple mixture and smooth over. Bake for 30 minutes, then remove from the oven and carefully arrange the lemon peel in a decorative pattern on top. Return to the oven for a further ten minutes until the pastry is golden and the filling set. Serve hot or cold. Serves 4-6.

Cumberland Sand Cake

Like Madeira Cake, Sand Cake was often served in Regency and Victorian days with a glass of wine – Madeira Cake with Madeira and Sand Cake with Sherry.

2 oz butter
4 oz caster sugar
2 eggs, beaten
1 oz flour
4 oz cornflour
1 level teaspoon baking powder
Pinch of salt
Pinch of grated nutmeg
2 teaspoons fresh lemon juice

Set oven to 350°F or Mark 4. Grease and line a 2 inch deep, 7 inch round cake tin. Cream the butter and sugar well together in a mixing bowl, add the eggs and beat well. Fold in the sieved flour, cornflour, baking powder, salt and nutmeg. Lastly add the lemon juice and mix well. Put in the tin and level the top. Bake for about 30 minutes until firm and golden. Leave in the tin for 15 minutes then turn out on to a wire rack. Dredge the top with a little sieved icing sugar.

Norfolk Plough Pudding

This pudding was traditionally served on Plough Monday, the first Monday after Twelfth Night, when spring ploughing was due to begin.

8 oz self-raising flour	**8 rashers streaky bacon, chopped**
A good pinch of salt	**1 large onion, peeled and chopped**
3 oz shredded suet	**1 teaspoon chopped sage**
1 lb pork sausagemeat	**½ oz brown sugar**

Water or pork stock

Mix the flour, salt and suet together then add sufficient cold water to form a soft dough. Turn out on to a lightly floured surface and roll out. Use ⅔ of the dough to line a greased 2 pint pudding basin, reserving the remaining ⅓ for the lid. Seal any gaps well and use the sausagemeat to line the dough, pressing them well together. Mix the bacon, onion, sage and sugar together and put in the basin, adding sufficient water or stock just to cover. Add the dough lid, pressing the edges firmly together and sealing with a little water. Cover with a circle of greaseproof paper and finally cover securely with kitchen foil. Cover and steam for 3½ to 4 hours. Serve with boiled potatoes and a selection of vegetables with thick brown gravy, served separately. Serves 4 to 6.

Feeding Ducks *by Arthur Claude Strachan*

Isle of Wight Doughnuts

These spicy doughnuts have a filling of currants rather than the usual red jam.

2 lb strong white flour
Pinch of salt
2 oz butter or lard
4 oz caster sugar
1 teaspoon allspice
Pinch of ground cloves
Pinch of ground nutmeg

½ pint milk
½ oz dried yeast
1½-2 oz currants
1 tablespoon sugar
¼ teaspoon cinnamon
Caster sugar mixed with a little ground cinnamon

Oil for frying

Sift the flour and salt together, then rub in the butter or lard until the mixture resembles fine breadcrumbs. Stir in the sugar and spices. Warm the milk, sprinkle over the yeast and leave until frothy. Add to the flour and stir to form a firm dough. Turn out on to a lightly floured surface and knead until smooth – about 10 minutes. Place in a bowl, cover with a clean teacloth and leave in a warm place for 1½ hours to rise. Then knock back and knead again. Form into balls about the size of a small apple. Mix the currants, sugar and cinnamon together, make a small hole in each doughnut, insert a few currants, then close up the hole. Leave in a warm place for 10 minutes. Heat the oil and deep-fry in small batches, turning once, until golden. Drain well on kitchen paper, then toss in the caster sugar mixture.

Rutland Savoury Cheese Custard

A traditional supper dish of grated cheese and eggs baked in a custard from England's smallest county.

6 oz well-flavoured Cheddar cheese, grated
2 eggs, beaten
¼ teaspoon dry mustard
Salt and black pepper
A few drops of Worcestershire Sauce – optional
2 oz butter
2 oz flour
½ pint milk
A little extra grated cheese

Set oven to 350°F or Mark 4. In a bowl, beat the grated cheese and eggs together, then add the seasoning and the Worcestershire Sauce, if desired. Melt the butter in a saucepan and stir in the flour, then gradually add the milk, stirring until the mixture boils and thickens. Stir into the cheese mixture, combining well, then turn into a 1½-2 pint buttered pie dish. Smooth over the top and sprinkle with the extra grated cheese. Bake for 15-20 minutes or until the custard is well-risen and golden. Serve immediately with triangles of buttered toast. Serves 4.

Feeding the Chickens *by Helen Allingham*

Yorkshire Pudding

Yorkshire pudding was traditionally served before the roast beef to take the edge off the appetite and make the meat go further. Today it is often served as an accompaniment to the meat. It should be light, crisp and just slightly soft in the middle and is at its best straight from the oven.

4 oz flour
¼ teaspoon salt
2 medium eggs
½ pint milk and water mixed
2 tablespoons beef dripping from the roasting tin

Prepare the batter by placing the flour and salt into a large bowl. Make a well in the centre and break the eggs into this. Using a wooden spoon or an electric whisk, beat the eggs and gradually add the milk and water, incorporating the flour a little at a time. Beat until the batter is smooth and leave to stand in a cool place for about one hour. Remove the roast beef from the oven and keep warm or transfer to a lower shelf. Raise the oven temperature to 425°F or Mark 7. Place the beef dripping in an 11 inch x 7 inch roasting tin and place in the oven until very hot, by which time the oven will have reached the higher temperature. Remove from the oven and pour the batter into the tin. Return to a high shelf in the oven and cook for approximately 25 minutes until risen, golden brown and crisp. Cut into squares and serve immediately.

Shropshire Fidget Pie

The name of this pie is said to come from the fact that it was originally 'fitched' or five-sided in shape.

3 medium potatoes, peeled and finely sliced
2 onions, peeled and sliced
2 cooking apples, peeled, cored and sliced
3 rashers sweetcure gammon, de-rinded and cut into strips
1½ oz butter
1 dessertspoon brown sugar
Salt and black pepper
½ teaspoon ground nutmeg
¼ pint pork or vegetable stock
8 oz prepared shortcrust pastry
Milk or beaten egg to glaze

Set oven to 350°F or Mark 4. Lightly fry the sliced potatoes, onions and apples in the butter until just golden. Remove with a slotted spoon and keep warm. Place the gammon in the pan and fry lightly in the remaining fat. Layer the gammon and the potatoes, onions and apples in a 1½-2 pint pie dish, seasoning with sugar, salt, pepper and nutmeg. Pour on the stock. On a lightly floured surface roll out the pastry and cover the pie, trimming the edges. Make a steam hole and decorate with the trimmings. Brush with milk or egg. Bake for 30 minutes, then reduce the oven to 325°F or Mark 3 for a further 10-15 minutes or until the pie is golden brown. Traditionally this pie is not served with vegetables, but carrots or cabbage can be served if desired. Serves 4-6.

Durham Pikelets

Pikelet is a regional name for a crumpet.

8 oz flour
1 teaspoon bicarbonate of soda
1 teaspoon cream of tartar
1½ oz lard
8-10 fl oz buttermilk or semi-skimmed milk
½ teaspoon salt

Sift the flour, bicarbonate of soda, cream of tartar and salt together into a bowl, then rub in the lard until the mixture resembles fine breadcrumbs. Make a well in the centre and add the buttermilk or milk, beating lightly to give a dropping consistency. Drop the mixture, in spoonfuls, on to a hot, well greased griddle or frying pan and cook the pikelets for about 4 minutes on each side until golden-brown. Keep warm, wrapped in a clean, warm tea towel and serve hot, spread with plenty of butter.

Berkshire Jugged Steak

A simple, but delicious recipe, that has its origins in the cauldron cookery of the Middle Ages, when a number of different dishes were boiled together in one large pot.

1½-2 lb rump steak
1 onion, peeled and left whole
10 cloves
2 carrots, peeled and diced
2 sticks celery, trimmed and diced
Salt and black pepper
1 or 2 teaspoons mushroom ketchup
3 sprigs parsley and a small bayleaf, tied together with a piece of kitchen string

Cut the steak into small, neat cubes and place in a tall, narrow casserole that has been rinsed out in cold water. Stick the onion with the cloves and add to the meat. Rinse the carrots and celery in cold water, drain well and add to the meat. Season, then add the mushroom ketchup and *bouquet garni*. Do *not* add any fat, stock or water. Cover the casserole with a piece of kitchen foil and place the lid firmly on top. Place in a saucepan of boiling water and stew for 2 hours, topping up the water as necessary. Before serving, discard the herbs and the cloves from the onion and then slice the onion and return it to the casserole. Serve with boiled potatoes and a green vegetable. Serves 4-6.

Off to Market *by Helen Allingham*

Nottingham Pudding

Also known as Apple-In-and-Out, this pudding dates back to medieval days, when a mixture of batter, fruit and spices was served with roast meat.

4 oz flour | **1 large egg** | **¼ pint water**
Pinch of salt | **¼ pint milk** | **1½-2 oz butter**

1 lb cooking apples, peeled, cored and sliced
Grated rind of half a lemon
2 teaspoons lemon juice
½ teaspoon ground cinnamon
3 oz brown sugar
1½-2 oz lard, for baking

Sift the flour and salt together in a bowl, make a well in the centre and stir in the egg, then gradually add half the milk and water, beating well until the batter is creamy. Add the remaining liquid and whisk the batter until smooth and light. Stand in a cool place for 20 minutes. Set oven to 425°F or Mark 7. Place the apples in melted butter in a heavy frying pan and add the lemon rind, juice, cinnamon and sugar. Cook gently until the apples are just soft. Put the lard in a 7½-8 inch square roasting tin and heat at the top of the oven until smoking. Very carefully arrange the apple mixture in the hot fat, then pour the batter over. Bake for 20 minutes, then reduce the oven temperature to 375°F or Mark 5 and bake for a further 20 minutes until the batter is firm and golden; because of the apple mixture, it will not rise as much as a plain batter. Serve with custard or cream. Serves 4-6.

Cheshire Soup

A cheese flavoured potato soup often served as a quick meal.

1 pint pork stock
10 oz potatoes, peeled and diced (weighed after peeling)
2 leeks, washed, trimmed and finely chopped
2 carrots, peeled and grated
Salt and black pepper
1 oz pinhead oatmeal
2 oz grated cheese, preferably Cheshire

Put the stock into a large saucepan, add the potatoes, leeks, carrots and seasoning and bring to the boil. Simmer for 15 minutes, or until the vegetables are soft. Sprinkle in the oatmeal and simmer for a further 10 minutes or until the soup has thickened. Just before serving, stir in half the cheese. Pour into 4 soup bowls, sprinkle on the remaining cheese and serve with crusty rolls or bread.

Going out to Play *by Helen Allingham*

Devonshire Splits

These sweet dough buns are often served with a traditional Clotted Cream tea. They are split and filled with the cream and home-made jam.

½ oz fresh yeast
1 teaspoon caster sugar
½ pint milk – warmed to blood heat
1 lb strong white flour
2 oz butter
1 oz caster sugar
1 teaspoon salt

Mix together the yeast, the teaspoon of sugar and the warm milk and leave in a warm place for 20-30 minutes until frothy. Rub the butter into the flour and stir in the 1 oz of sugar and the salt. Add the yeast liquid to the flour and mix to a soft dough. Knead on a floured surface until smooth and elastic. Leave covered in a warm place for about 1 hour until doubled in size. Knock back, knead again and divide into 16 pieces. Mould into neat bun shapes and place on floured baking sheets. Leave once again in a warm place until well risen. Bake in a pre-heated oven at 425°F or Mark 7 for approximately 15 minutes until pale golden in colour. Cool on a wire rack.

Hampshire Haslet

Haslet comes from the Old French word for entrails, but basically refers to the fact that all the ingredients are very finely minced.

8 oz stale white bread, cubed
Milk or water for soaking
2 lb lean pork, coarsely minced
1 medium onion, peeled and chopped
1 teaspoon fresh chopped sage
Salt and black pepper

Soak the bread in sufficient milk or water to cover and, when soft, squeeze out the excess moisture. Set the oven to 375°F or Mark 5. Mix together the bread, pork, onion, sage and seasoning. Put through a fine mincer. Lightly grease a 2½-3 lb loaf tin. Put the mixture into the tin and press down firmly and evenly. Bake for 1½-2 hours, covering the top with kitchen foil if it browns too quickly. Allow to cool slightly in the tin, then turn out and allow to cool completely. Serve cold, sliced, with salad and boiled potatoes. Serves 4-6.

Kentish Apple and Cheese Pie

This recipe comes from the Garden of England, renowned for its apple orchards and beloved by Charles Dickens.

6 oz puff or shortcrust pastry
1½ lb cooking apples, peeled, cored and thickly sliced
3-4 oz granulated sugar
3-4 cloves
Small pinch of grated nutmeg
½ teacup of water
4 oz hard cheese, sliced

Set oven to 425°F or Mark 7. Grease an 8 inch (approx.) pie dish. Using half the apples, put a layer into the dish and sprinkle half the sugar over. Lay the remaining apples on top and push the cloves into some of the apple slices. Add the remaining sugar, the nutmeg and the water and make a final layer with the cheese. Roll out the pastry on a lightly floured surface and use it to cover the dish; trim and decorate. Brush with a little milk to glaze and bake for approximately 40-45 minutes. Serves 4-6.

METRIC CONVERSIONS

The weights, measures and oven temperatures used in the preceding recipes can be easily converted to their metric equivalents.

Weights

Avoirdupois	Metric
1 oz.	just under 30 grams
4 oz. (¼ lb.)	app. 115 grams
8 oz. (½ lb.)	app. 230 grams
1 lb.	454 grams

Liquid Measures

Imperial	Metric
1 tablespoon (liquid only)	20 millilitres
1 fl. oz.	app. 30 millilitres
1 gill (¼ pt.)	app. 145 millilitres
½ pt.	app. 285 millilitres
1 pt.	app. 570 millilitres
1 qt.	app. 1.140 litres

Oven Temperatures

	°Fahrenheit	Gas Mark	°Celsius
Slow	300	2	140
	325	3	158
Moderate	350	4	177
	375	5	190
	400	6	204
Hot	425	7	214
	450	8	232
	500	9	260

Flour as specified in these recipes refers to Plain Flour unless otherwise described.